PEOPLE WHO LIKE MEATBALLS

Selima Hill grew up in a family of painters in farms in England and Wales, and has lived in Dorset for the past 30 years. She won first prize in the Arvon/*Observer* International Poetry Competition with part of *The Accumulation of Small Acts of Kindness* (1989), one of several extended sequences in *Gloria: Selected Poems* (Bloodaxe Books, 2008). *Gloria* includes work from *Saying Hello at the Station* (1984), *My Darling Camel* (1988), *A Little Book of Meat* (1993), *Aeroplanes of the World* (1994), *Violet* (1997), *Bunny* (2001), *Portrait of My Lover as a Horse* (2002), *Lou-Lou* (2004) and *Red Roses* (2006). Her latest collections from Bloodaxe are *The Hat* (2008), *Fruitcake* (2009), and *People Who Like Meatballs* (2012), shortlisted for both the Forward Poetry Prize and the Costa Poetry Award.

Violet was a Poetry Book Society Choice and was short-listed for all three of the UK's major poetry prizes, the Forward Prize, T.S. Eliot Prize and Whitbread Poetry Award. *Bunny* won the Whitbread Poetry Award, was a Poetry Book Society Choice and was shortlisted for the T.S. Eliot Prize. *Lou-Lou* and *The Hat* were Poetry Book Society Recommendations. She was given a Cholmondeley Award in 1986, and was a Royal Literary Fund Fellow at the University of Exeter in 2003-06.

As a tutor, Selima Hill has worked in prisons, hospitals and monasteries as well as for the Arvon Foundation and London's South Bank Centre. She has worked on several collaborations with artists including: *Parched Swallows* with choreographer Emily Claid; *Point of Entry* with sculptor Bill Woodrow; and *Trembling Hearts in the Bodies of Rocks* with performance artist Ilona Medved-Lost.

SELIMA HILL

PEOPLE WHO LIKE MEATBALLS

BLOODAXE BOOKS

Copyright © Selima Hill 2012

ISBN: 978 1 85224 945 8

First published 2012 by
Bloodaxe Books Ltd,
Highgreen,
Tarset,
Northumberland NE48 1RP.

Second impression 2012.

www.bloodaxebooks.com
For further information about Bloodaxe titles
please visit our website or write to
the above address for a catalogue.

Supported using public funding by
**ARTS COUNCIL
ENGLAND**

Cover design: Neil Astley & Pamela Robertson-Pearce.

Printed in Great Britain by
Bell & Bain Limited, Glasgow, Scotland.

For comfort I went at once to my friends the Javelles and was invited to join them for lunch in the cupboard behind the shop; rather crowded as they already had one guest. They were in cheerful mood, revived by the death of Claude Buffet, the bookseller brother of the artist and a frequent visitor to their shop. I may have reported one of my meetings with him there years ago. We were all gathered at the shop at the end of a day that I had spent at a book-fair. I complained that there were not enough books and too many postcards. We expounded on the absurdity of postcards and their collectors. Claude Javelle told us about a man who came every day to the shop to ask if she had any postcards of elephants. There was an odd silence and then M. Buffet asked indignantly, 'What's so funny about elephants?'

DAVID BATTERHAM
Among Booksellers (Stone Trough Books, 2011)

CONTENTS

People Who Like Meatballs

Into My Mother's Snow-Encrusted Lap

PEOPLE WHO LIKE MEATBALLS

Modest Acts of Extreme Slowness

I thought you were nice,
I thought it was all my fault;
I thought it was all my fault right from the beginning
and nothing really mattered except you,
I thought you were Mr Right
but I was wrong;
I thought you could play the piano but I was wrong,
I thought that being attractive wasn't important
as long as you played the piano but I was wrong;

I thought I could somehow entrust you with my body
like golden soup entrusted to warmed bowls,
that if I grabbed your head and whacked or slapped it
it'd change your ways; that men will always thank me;
that married couples in their beds perform
modest acts of extreme slowness;
that making love with you would be the same
as making love with lots of little kittens;
I thought I heard them purring. I was wrong.

Parkdirektor Riggers

Can't you understand that all is well,
that people are much nicer than you think,
that those who maintain that you've definitely got to repent
before you can be forgiven are definitely right,
that mothers love to bake delicious cakes;
that no one cares; that Christ is not an elephant;
that swimming after meals can be dangerous;
that every immediate moment is dynamic,
giddy, afflicted, diffident and obscured;

that having a little telly in your kitchen
that neatly unfolds from your units makes perfect sense,
that the man who steps out of the window has got to be joking,
that ultrasweatproof deodorant's ultrasweatproof,
that to name a rose *Parkdirektor Riggers*
also makes perfect sense; that all is lost;
that outer space is on the point of bursting;
that choosing a Bugaboo pushchair says it all;
that Béla Tarr is boring? Nor can I.

Arithmetic

It's time you learnt to learn that I'm not suitable,
that a kiss from me is no more uplifting than duck's blood,
that I'd rather be doing arithmetic in the woods

than having sex with you which I find distressing
whereas being bored is easy and boring and nice
but having sex with you is just distressing.

Nasty Little Moments on Park Benches

There's no such thing as saying no to sleep,
as the crushed and dismembered miners not being loved,
as you not being loved, as humorous doormats,
as surviving on peas and sardines,
as correct spelling,
as surviving on raspberries and sausages sprinkled with sugar,
as you and me,
as happy ever after,
as the red-faced flasher being a lepidopterist,
as crying for who or what we want to cry for,
as a woman with thirty-six breasts,
as beautiful feet;
as *imperturbable and serene composure*;

as people who kindly stop talking for long enough so you can
        ask them
to please stop; as constancy; as excessive joy;
as travelling by minibus all the way to the seaside
to sit with your back to the sea; as Elvis Presley;
as proof that God does not exist,
as wurk,
as nasty little moments on park benches
turning out OK, as bleeped-out rants,
as going to all that trouble, as perfect diction,
as not being thrown by the solitariness of desire,
as finding love in a cabin you call WY-WURK;
there's no such thing as appeasing your inmost desires;
as an end to pain and suffering; as Mamma.

Living, Breathing Lumbar Rolls and Wedges

I'm bored of having skin like pink flowers
and bored of having breasts I can't lie down on
and hair that's like a hat made of scourers
and what I need's a proper pair of ears,
enormous, heart-shaped, shadow-coloured ears
that move like herons in a blue haze
where trees and ghosts of trees and ghosts of lily-trotters

have to be believed to be believed;
I'm bored of being me, I need to roll,
to wrap myself in mud like a hog,
to wrap myself in sunsets, to be leant against
like living, breathing lumbar rolls and wedges;
to roll along as slowly as an aeroplane
made of semolina with a face

as sweet as only faces made of nutmeg
and creamy semolina can be sweet;
to roll in jewels till I fall asleep –
in other words, I want to be an elephant,
or what I think it's like to be an elephant,
an elephant who'll never know it's me
and wouldn't dream of being small or pink.

Fun

Because you seem to think it's fun to whimper,
fun to be an unctuous little squit,
someone one can pop between one's fingernails
to watch it die its small affronted death;
fun to whine non-stop like a mosquito
tangled in the tangles of the hair
I've dipped like an enormous ewe in something
you obviously can't stop yourself inhaling,

fun to splutter, fun to not be needed,
fun to be abandoned like a racehorse
abandoned by everything but flies,
fun to be a fly, to live on dung;
because you seem to think it's fun to beg me,
on bended knee, for pity's sake, to love you,
would you be offended if I asked you
to think about something else for a change?

Muriel

I used to have a tadpole I called Muriel
who'd look me in the eye as if to say

Give me back my pond, my lovely pondweed,
give me back my jellied palisades,

give me back whatever...then she died,
too small, too cold, too slimy to survive;

anyhow you too are much too small
and I'm ashamed to even have to look at you.

Drop Dead Gorgeous and a Billionaire

Because I've never found the perfect man
who's drop-dead gorgeous and billionaire
and loves to help and owns so many elephants
he wouldn't mind a bit if one was mine,
not one bit – he'd show us where to go,
where to find the sweetest plums and raspberries,
the sand-baths and the mud-baths and the lilies,
and, best of all, the lake where the elephant
will take me for a ride on his back

and when the water gets too deep to paddle in
we'll gradually find ourselves swimming
and as our bodies slowly rise and fall
the sun, the lake, the fish will disappear
till nothing moves except the big grey feet
moving forward on behalf of everything...
but anyway, as I said before,
because I've never found such a man
I'm having to content myself with you.

It's Got So Hot You Can't Even Speak

It's got so hot you can't even speak
and the only sound is the sound of a high-pitched buzzing
that seems to come from how you can't stand up

and how you're not a man but a pylon
that's found itself sitting on my lawn
in a very hot and uncomfortable position.

Traces of Skin From Your Neck

I'm riding along with my boots full of blood and a gun
and traces of skin from your neck tucked under my nails
and I'm finding it really hard not to gloat
and I'm riding along in the glow of a beautiful sunset
and I'm dreaming of you and I'm dreaming of you being dead
and I'm finding it really hard not to scream,
like really really hard, like a yogi
who's only allowed to eat feather dusters:
Please can I breathe! Please can I *not* have a man!

Please can I not have a man of any description,
least of all a man who looks like you
and sounds like and smells like you and *is* you
and please can I have an elephant instead
and please can I also have a hot savannah,
a pink one, with some tamarind bushes
dotted here and there and a lake
in which we'll swim as languidly as willow trees
changing their position in their sleep.

Never Be Alone in a Heatwave

When it gets so hot you can't sleep
or even breathe, when you think you'll die –
and having sex with someone when you're sleepy
is hard enough, as we all know,
but having sex with someone when you're dead
is really really hard but anyway
at least when someone's dead they can forget
that all the really terrible things that happen
always seem to happen in a heatwave! –
never be afraid to say no.
Never sleep with someone when you're sweaty
and grains of grit dot the sheets like barnacles

and all you want to do is be a lettuce leaf
or go and find a frozen lake somewhere
to roll around the surface with no clothes on on
until you stick and turn an icy blue;
so never sleep with someone in a heatwave
– but also never be alone in one either
because what happens is you stop eating,
you don't know how to speak, or who you are,
cats go missing, flowers turn to dust,
birds give up and fall from the sky
and darkness settles on the little garage
in which your body slumps as if in prayer.

I Couldn't Stand the Smell of the Pinks

I couldn't stand the smell of the pinks
and I honestly used to think I was going crazy

and I probably *did* go crazy in a way
because during the day I was terrified of the night

and during the night I was terrified of the day
and then in the *day* I was terrified of the *day*

so probably, yes, I did go a little crazy
and that was when the elephant appeared,

colossal and refulgent, at my side
(colossal but without any fuss)

and soon we started walking down the road,
nice and slow, like people carrying buckets.

The Most Beautiful Woman in
the History of Lawn Tennis

At night we reinvent ourselves as moths
that can't remember, if they ever knew,

how to be alive or who they are
or where there is to crawl to except hair,

that think they know what Love is
but they don't,

no one does, it is unknowable,
along with everything else, including me;

including things in zoos that can't be bred from
or ever kept alive, that bite their keepers;

including tongues, and the gift of tongues,
and bedding that's not wet and doesn't move;

including the ex-dancer you're convinced
is the most beautiful woman in the history of lawn tennis.

The Elephant Is Much Too Big to Boogie

The elephant is much too big to boogie
and when I see him standing there like that
he makes me feel very nice and peaceful
like sobbing does when you sob and sob:
so ponderous and dim, he just stands there,
inert not with inertia but with love!
(The elephant is much too big to wink
but when he looks at me he almost does...)

Like summer days when nothing wants to move,
like wardrobes full of sleeping bags, the elephant
has gone to sleep without lying down,
he doesn't need to bother, he's got bones
specially made to double as a bed
for if you want to sleep standing up,
to close your eyes and let enormous planets
roll towards you like delicious buns.

Snow-white Katarinas

I want the bony head, I want the back –
as wide and empty as a drawing-room,
a drawing-room or ballroom in a palace
where nothing ever happens except beetles
walking in and out of squares of light –
the elongated nose so I can wave
to passing aunts and uncles as they sway,
as big and white as snow-white Katarinas
in and out of loops of dappled shade;

I want to be a humble gyrovague
and spending my days wandering in circles
in and out of lakes – what's wrong with that?
I want to be a huge and saggy elephant –
but not because an elephant is huge
but *how* he's huge, the way he moves about
and walks across the grass as if the grass
is giving him a lesson in lucidity;
an elephant who doesn't need a home,

who walks along to walk along, that's all,
dipping in and out of grass like tongues
dipping in and out of liqueur;
I want his shiny eyes like new-born mice;
I want the way he dances, like a barn,
his sunflower-crunching trunk-enhancing barn-dance;
I want to be an elephant and not
the tiniest and most something little something
it's ever been God's privilege to ruin.

Everything He Touches Turns to Gold

Everything he touches turns to gold –
my arms, my hips, the winceyette pyjamas
that feel as if a thousand little moths
have settled on my skin in their sleep –
all solid gold; I can't move a thing

and all I do is watch as the elephant
leans himself against me like the moon
and lets my body shimmer in the eyes
that stare at me as if they still remember
who we were before the world began.

The Graceful Swaying of the Elephant

The graceful swaying of the elephant –
an elephant who doesn't want to know
he tramples forests underfoot like sausages
and chomps his way through entire citrus farms
with bones and teeth like solid billiard balls
while churning up great clouds of dust like monuments
falling in the squares of the damned –

the diligent and humble way he ambles
back and forth along the sleepy trails
as if there's nowhere he would rather be
seems to be God's charming way of saying –
typically obscure, if not nonsensical! –
the elephant on whose back I'm riding
is made of hymns (ancient and modern).

It's Easy To Be Lazy When You're Lazy

It's easy to be lazy when you're lazy
and it's easy to be lazy when you're huge,
to drift on tiptoe like an ungulate
on big grey feet,
to dine on passing trees,
to whisk my little fly-whisk in the sun,
to casually impersonate a cube;
to move as if one's made of someone's eyelashes,
grave and imperturbable; to breathe
very slowly like a mother rose
or someone on whose shoulder men break down;

to shamble through the groves of orange marigolds
as lazily as a giant pie,
as waterfalls and hyacinths and hyacinth farms
wrapped in sacks, as quadrupedal sea-cows;
a diffident, balletic, incorruptible
silver rubber wedding-dress with ears
and elongated teeth made of piano keys;
to shamble through the marigolds so lazily,
so half-asleep, it's easy to forget
an elephant will always be an elephant
and I will always never not be me.

Entire Courts Together with Their Kings

The elephant who's standing on my foot,
who smiles like a pile of full moons
or an excited king in a pair of velvet slippers
tiptoeing through the woods for the last time,
whose presence has the same sedating effect
as sacred texts on someone no one's noticed
has been unhappy for nearly fifty years;

the elephant, like a religious order
making its way through an unsuspecting world
on big grey feet, his eyes like millet seed;
whose tender meat the colour of stocks and lupins
is overjoyed to be so huge and meaty;
the elephant, like a prudent beetle
crawling across the lens of someone's spectacles,

across their ear, across their epaulette,
across vast courts together with their kings;
the elephant, who God Himself has made
in order to be loved by Him, the elephant
takes no notice of me whatsoever –
or that's what you might think but that's because
it's no big deal: he and I know that.

Sixteen Reasons for Being a Nun

The elephant is perfectly content
with only ever knowing what he knows –
with how to peel fruit and how to trumpet
and how to go to sleep in a desert
where nothing really matters except love
and where to go to sleep in a desert
where nothing really matters except love
and where to find a nice acacia-tree
and what will be inside it when he finds it

and what the sixteen reasons for being a nun are
(some so easy, some so very hard!)
and how to meet the Maker face to face
who in His wisdom made Jake Gyllenhaal
and also made (as if that wasn't enough!)
hot house flowers the size of Arizona
to perfume him and pile at his feet –
but no one knows if being good is meaningless
in itself, least of all the elephant.

The Entire Universe and All Its Precious Contents

You may be many things but big's not one of them –
you're more the size of one of those weird spiders

that hide away in dens and dine alone
on the still-living bodies of full-bloodied paralysed caterpillars –

but also can I say something else:
the elephant is actually *not big*!

The elephant is simply being an elephant
and elephants are always correctly-sized

along with the entire correctly-sized universe
and all its precious correctly-sized contents

including the deep thick rim of dark blue light
which I don't understand; which is called the Feynman point;

which, far from being deaf, is, even now,
waiting in the heavens to be called –

though why, by whom, for what, I've no idea.
Things like that tend to get kept secret.

The Elephant Whose Sturgeon-like Blood

The elephant whose sturgeon-like blood
insists it was or ought to be aquatic,
whose ears, like hairy crackle-glazed chopping boards,
are cheerfully agreeing to be fans,
fingers his marulas with a trunk
strong enough to paralyse a tiger,
a trunk that's been wired up with special nerves
found nowhere else except the clitoris,
a trunk whose full-time job is being free
with the slightly anarchic freedom of uncertainty;
that spends its life seeing what it's like
to live as both an arm and a nose,

a trunk that never stops embracing homelessness
even while it's guiding the elephant
past the sandy smells of sons and daughters
that smell of banks of pinks and carnations
and in and out of sand dunes and ant-hills
glittering with dew and small beetles
and down towards the water where the crocodiles,
(that think they are unworthy, like Judas,
of being, of deserving to be, good)
are not as fast asleep as we think they are,
a trunk whose every nerve aspires to homelessness
even while it leads him safely home.

The Ugly Ones

You couldn't give a shit about the elephant –
the way it walks, the way it keeps on walking,
the way it's like there's no such thing as walking,

no such thing as feet, or the absence of feet,
no such thing as nothing any more
and no such thing as so-called drop-dead-gorgeous –

but anyway who cares, I like the ugly ones,
the ones with ears as big as Africa
for generating nice cooling breezes,

who walk along so slowly it looks easy
but even when you're walking at your slowest
you walk along too fast to know it's not.

Jonquil

A jonquil is a jonquil-coloured finch;
Omelette is the name of my first hen;

sunsets look like corrugated goldfish
and sometimes I am kind but not always.

Never Trust a Clock That Tells the Time

How nice to not be able to be lost,
to sleep on foot, to be your own home;

to never leave, to never not be here,
to live the lie that leaving is arriving;

how nice to have – to be! – a friendly clock
that tells the time in ticks and tocks that tell you

to never trust a clock that tells the time
and, when you take your bath, to take your bath

as slowly as you possibly can
because it's not a bath but a mud-bath

and time is not and never will be time.

The Quality of My Adoration

Something like a sofa made of buns
is settling itself backwards on my lap –
or trying to: it doesn't understand
it's not a baby, it's an elephant,
not to mention warble-flies, so, no,
it's never going to work, I'm afraid,
much as I would like to say it will,
much as I would like – would love! – to cuddle him,

to gaze into his little seed-like eyes
and kiss his scratchy cheek, but it won't work;
being sort of sat on by a sofa –
a large unhappy sofa with a tail,
that dreams of growing up to be a ship
whose wake of gold will grasp the sea and hurtle it
out across the sky until it shatters
and showers us with jewels – doesn't work,

is never going to work, but the elephant,
refusing to accept that his behind
is not a perfect fit, the sobbing elephant
seems to think *I've ruined his life* –
which only goes to show how wrong I was
to think, to even dream, that an elephant
could possibly begin to understand
the quality of my adoration.

Never Trust a Man without an Elephant

Never leave the house without a handkerchief,
never eat unless you're sitting down,
never coat your head in gold and honey
and never be afraid to spell Beuys,
never doubt the story that the Rift Valley
one dark night gave birth to the moon
and never, day or night, disturb the women
diligently breast-feeding soldiers;

never hope a quiet newt will holler,
never clean tin pans without rhubarb
and never look an elephant in the eye;
and while you understand you'll pass away,
always live as though you think you won't;
but life is even shorter than you thought
and every day is like a van or lorry
full of chandeliers in fragile boxes

driven by a driver who's so cool
he wears a garnet nose-stud in his nose
and keeps his kids in cigarettes and Pringles
and no, he doesn't cuddle them, he beats them
so every day let's thank the Lord we know
that those who want a long and happy life
should never trust a man who's got no elephant
but only drives a lorry or a van.

Fruit

I only want to talk about fruit,
large and small and medium-sized fruit,
and never the so-called lover I never loved,

the lover I refuse to be a lover of,
who being with is hating every minute of,
whose body is what hair and hair-dos have,

whose cosy so-called bedroom's so-called bed
is no more cosy than a new pin;
not him, not hair, not cosy rooms: fruit.

Midnight

Everyone's asleep except the elephant
who stands beside my bed in the dark

as if to show the world what would happen
if someone crossed a saint with a potato.

Never Be Alone with a Moth

Never start the day without a grapefruit –
and never be awake unless you're clean,
unless your home's as clean as a whistle;
never think a maid will come along
and help you with the washing-up, she won't;
never be alone with a moth;
never go a day without chocolate,
and hide enough supplies in drawers and boxes
to keep you going when you can't sleep,

when hundreds and thousands of moths appear from
nowhere
and creep across your face like freeze-dried kittens
and down your neck and up and down your hair,
trying not to panic as they knead
a secret place to push through and emerge,
redeemed, triumphant, if a little dusty,
into a world of light, or being loved,
of having lovers falling at one's feet
(by 'lovers' I mean mist, I mean silk,

I mean the softest quadrupeds, like chocolate drops,
or Vaseline, I mean a certain elephant:
I see him now, kneeling at my feet,
O my God, how huge I must be
to have my own aurora borealis clone
here on earth kneeling at my feet)
so, never start the day without a grapefruit
and, on the grapefruit, one on each half,
never start the day without two cherries.

Strangers

I like the way they can't pronounce my name,
I like the way their arms are so bony

they couldn't even hug me if they tried
and I like the way they *go away*, like newly-weds

who've got their own mysterious lives to lead,
to leave the house with, like mysterious dogs;

who meet in groups or on their own in bars
I'm free to feel I haven't got to join them in,

all wearing clothes I can't believe they're wearing
and eating food I can't believe they eat –

meatballs, for example, or profiteroles –
and most of all I like the way, with strangers,

that, inasmuch as *you* are different from *me*,
I am different from *you* – so we're the same!

Please Can I Have a Man and Two Children

Please can I have a man and two children
and please can I have a face like Alek Wek

and please can I have a body like Heidi Klum
and please can I have an amicable divorce

and please can I have the organic deep-fried pea-pods
and (here we go again) a friendly elephant –

a large or small or medium-sized elephant
that will or won't provide me with a hair

to make myself an elephant-hair bracelet with,
a chocolate-coloured hair; and if not why not?

The Fly

The thought of being someone else's thought –
of being someone someone else is pining for,
someone else tiptoeing about
and getting on my nerves, who never stops,
who never stops long enough to know

what it is he's stopping for, or pining for,
who needs to look about him, like the plantigrade
(the elephant, the wolverine, the bear)
the soles of whose wide feet resemble picnic-rugs
spread on sunny days at grassy picnic-spots –

the thought of being thought about by someone
is like an unborn fly in my brain
that keeps me from whatever lies ahead,
from everything that's being asked of me,
that seems to be, at the same time, offered.

Out on the Shimmering Lake
by the Dark Plantations

I'll never forget the night a large elephant
burst into my bedroom like a pig,
flabby-fleshed and talkative, but then
I'd never been alone like that before;

I lived my life like someone in a dogsuit
alternately chained to my chain or chained to a rowlock
out on the shimmering lake by the dark plantations;
hunting, being hunted; marble-hearted;

with not a clue how not to be afraid,
afraid of being loved, I think I mean:
I'd never been alone with an elephant
knee-deep in plantains and knee-deep in grace.

One of God's Delicious Home-made Beetles

Because your face is like the sort of pie
that people eat who never eat anything,
that's frankly too unappetising-looking,
too cold to even nibble at or suck,
that makes one want to chuck it in the bin;
because your smile, like a homesick fish,
is something I refuse to feel touched by,
because you run around like little boys
who clutch their little guns and run and run

smack into the trumpets of huge flowers
and lie there, kicking and screaming in wet boxer-shorts,
incapable of joy, till someone comes;
because you are beside yourself with longing,
your mother may have loved you – but not me:
whenever you exhaust yourself with staring at me,
with longing for me like a helpless fish
for one of God's delicious home-made beetles,
I'm sorry but I can't even look.

Never Go to Sleep While You're Driving

Never go to sleep while you're driving
and never drive a car when you're dead
and if you meet a fish on a bicycle
never even think they're man and wife.

Lily Bulbs

They're waiting in the fridge for a lake,
for heatwaves, giant butterflies and elephants

who know there's no such thing as being lazy;
that muddy water's perfect for the ears;

that if you are a woman you need chocolate
and if you are a lily bulb, mud,

and, if you are an elephant, the bliss
of never having heard of gymnastics.

The Little Girl

Let's feast ourselves on plums until we're sick
and totally incapable of anything
except of giving in to the dream

in which I am a little girl again –
or not so little, maybe nine or ten,
maybe 'little' for the last time –

who lies abandoned in the empty house
and feels in her blood, like a stone,
the violence of having been adored,

a violence that rolls along so tenderly
that, even as it frightens her, she's feeling it
bear her sorrows ceaselessly away.

Flank-sucker

Because they've never heard the ominous sound
of tiny children and enormous clocks,
because they've never even heard of clocks,
because they wear inflatable shoes for feet;
because they don't need anything new to happen,
and heat is just a jelly they're suspended in;
because they wisely spare themselves surprises
by sticking with their friends like sleepy pears,
because their hands are noses and sniff everything –
even me who nobody dares touch! –

because I'm too excited by their touch
to bother to be humble anymore,
to bother to sit still and stay indoors
(like Dobermans in cages who flank-suck;
sows who chew their bars; crated voles
who jump and jump their little feet right off;
like bears in zoos who swing their heads like buckets)
I peel off my little knee-length dress
and praise the god of elephants for elephants –
and may the hare-brained god of me praise me!

Zoos at Night

The disappearance of pigs from the British landscape;
Patsy Cline, Patsy Cline's shrimp salad,
the plane, the scream, the all-engulfing swamps;

the Walkaloosa doing what it's told;
apricot linoleum, fawn cardigans,
zoos at night – or what? I dread to think

what it must be like to be like you,
in floods of tears twenty times a day;
not even that; just wishing that you were.

The Ritual Funerals of Broken
Sewing-machine Needles

The ritual funerals of broken sewing-machine needles –
the velvet cushions and the twinkling lights –

that celebrate not only the needles
but also those who celebrate the needles,

broken at their hands, as you are broken,
are funerals only cynics could resist.

The Swimmer

Everything's been turned into slits
and if I swim out far enough I too

can join the other slits that spend the day
sliding into each other and exploding.

Chukk-a-Ball

His itchy wings keep getting in the way,
his feet are huge, his eggs are like huge lamp-shades,

he smells of fudge and eats like a horse
and when he tries to chuck his stupid Chukk-a-Ball

his feathers get entangled in his halo
and now he says he's getting so fed up

he begs to not be dreamt; to not be mine;
to be a proper elephant who mates.

Just Because You Wear Those Ridiculous Clothes

Just because you wear those ridiculous clothes
and love yourself so much it's actually frightening,
just because you wear those ridiculous clothes
while having sex here, there and everywhere
all night long with anything that moves;
just because it's your idea of fun
to jump around the bedroom like a frog
who's not so much a frog as a tadpole;
who's much too dim to know that frogs are pondlife
and no one needs to know about pondlife;

because you fall like socks at my feet;
because you simply haven't got a clue,
not a clue, and no one's about to tell you,
of course they're not, they can't, they're much too busy
searching for the perfect piece for layering
the perfect layer for their 'sleeve-less look';
just because you've *got* no look – like roadkill
that lorries kill again and again,
just because the socks you used to wear
to tiptoe to my bed in bulge with mice

and the big red lips that sent shivers down your spine
send shivers down the spine of someone else
and when you see me coming now you wince
as if you're someone's wound and I am iodine,
and just because we don't know what to say
or even how to smile anymore
because we are afraid and there's too much

that can or can't be said and it's too late;
because we talk as if we're wrapped in tulle
whose tiny little skin-tight mouths are praying,

if we talk at all;
because we don't talk,
because I dream I want to be a cube
experiencing nothing but straight lines
and when it's just the elephant and me
and everything goes quiet and the elephant
leans against my arm as if to say
he needs me to protect him from the bees
even though there are no bees and anyhow
the elephant's much bigger than I am

and both of us –
the elephant and me –
know we only have to do nothing
and stillness will express itself itself;
just because it's just the two of us –
the elephant and me – and just because,
just because there's no such thing as mercy
and I never want to see you again,
it doesn't mean to say that I don't love you
and neither does it mean to say I do.

Thank You for the Word on Everyone's Lips

Thank you for the word on everyone's lips
and thank you for the heroically-struck high C,

for chocolate buttons, cowslips, speleologists,
for tulips you can tiptoe through, for Tide;

and thank you for Jake Gyllenhaal and thank you
for the thought of Jake Gyllenhaal drenched in his favourite
        Mitsuki

being here on earth to help others
though what the others are here for no one knows

nor do we know who it is who I'm suddenly thanking
but anyhow I thank you, I thank you

for chocolate buttons but also chocolate drops,
for time, for space, and for the ukulele

(and for all the men and women like myself
who get it a bit confused at times with the banjo).

God Bless Lower Alcohol Pina Colada

I used to have a cockatoo called Buttercup
or Butterfly or Butterscotch or anyway
something yellow, everything was yellow:
the chopped-up boiled eggs, the chopped-egg salad,
milk, bile, buttercups, the river
full of petals, cowshit, yellow fish,
into which I plunged like a lunatic
in order to escape from certain people
who couldn't bring themselves to stop grumbling,
who grumbled all the time, beat people up –

beat the living daylights out of people,
even beat the daylights out of daylight –
tell me if you don't understand –
I'm talking about yellow – heat, grain –
I'm trying to be direct but it's not easy:
the men, OK, the men and their women
who got on each other's nerves at the slightest thing,
whose faces were red as the faces of top-level saints,
whose words, when they spoke, were the names of the horses
          at Ascot,
who were soothed by reciting the names of the horses at Ascot,

who fed me shredded wheat like beheaded shrews
or the chopped-up stick-nests of the Hammerkop
or the hide-outs of rats in coconut plantations
and I'm talking about going swimming: may God bless swimming!
And bless the ocean (the so-called Fremantle doctor!)
bless the hose, bless the cattle-trough,

bless the Winey Keemun, bless the milk,
bless my Lower Alcohol Pina Colada
and God bless thirst and the quenching of thirst and summertime
and – tell me if I'm boring you – front crawl.

INTO MY MOTHER'S SNOW-ENCRUSTED LAP

Into My Mother's Snow-Encrusted Lap

Into my mother's snow-encrusted lap
I throw my little ping-pong ball – but no,

she doesn't throw it back, she's much too busy
sharpening her snow-encrusted axe.

Chickenshit

Chickenshit! chickenshit! chickenshit!
Everywhere you look – just God and chickenshit,

and sometimes you can hear Him pacing about
or sense a glow as if between old floorboards

but mostly all you see and hear is chickenshit –
and chickenshit is worse than you think!

My Mother's Friends

Dressed in gauntlets and enormous boots
and sweating like a pig, she's chopping wood;
she chops and chops until she's too exhausted
and much too hot to even keep her clothes on
and when she isn't chopping she is diving,
crashing from the jetty with such force
she almost turns the lake inside out,

leaving me alone on the bank
to burrow into tunnels of her underwear
and practise being someone dressed in silk
but all too soon she's back and chopping wood
although it's much too hot to be chopping
but anyhow my mother's much too busy
to sit around wasting time with friends.

Among the Butterflies

I'm lying on my back among the butterflies,
manifesting as the perfect hedgerow.

My Mother's Foot

My mother's much too tall to be a mother
but lets me dream she lets me have a foot:

she lets me rest my chin against her foot
and marvel at the sheen of her warts

and lets me clamber up across the ankle
planted in my bog like a door-jamb.

Hugging

As a boat is said to "hug" the coast –
creeping slowly forward where the rocks

sway below the bows like a city
the tiny person in the tiny boat

mustn't get too close to, yet calls Home –
so could I be said to "hug" my mother.

Caterpillars

Hundreds of the cabbage-white caterpillars
that live inside the cabbages the cabbage-lorries

crunch to pieces in the cabbage-fields
turn not into butterflies but mush.

Walrus

She isn't where she was and where she ought to be
but somewhere else entirely altogether

with someone with a tongue like a walrus
who wants to stuff her head into his mouth.

Even the Obedient Brown Horses

Even the obedient brown horses
walk the other way when my mother

buttons up her yellow winter coat
with hands she's trained like thugs to mete out pain.

The Shimmering Lake

It's midnight when my mother and I
swim together for the last time

and as we swim
we have the strange sensation

we're swimming in the lake of someone's mind
although of course we know

there is no someone
and drowning isn't drowning either too.

Stallions

You have to wonder is this person fit
to be a mother, anybody's mother,

and yes, I'm meaning mine in particular,
after all, I'm still her son, you know,

the blueness of whose eyes course through her veins
like God's own blood that courses through the veins

of floral-spangled fillies in cool vales
and floral-spangled foals and blue-eyed stallions.

Everyone Is Wearing Tiny Shorts

Everyone is wearing tiny shorts –
everyone, that is, except my mother

who wears a pair of shit-caked dungarees
bleached and stiff from years of striding about

in and out of blocks of blazing sunlight
slapping bullocks' rumps and kneeing goats

that stare at her with eyes that glint like rum
with which she dreams her cup runneth over.

My Mother's Nose

My mother with a plaster on her nose
briskly spraying breast-milk at the greenfly,
far from being inspirational,
depresses me – can you understand that?

I breakfast to the sound of the crunch
of powder compacts underfoot like crabs,
above my chair the figure of an angel
dressed from head to toe in white leather.

Black Against the Sky, the Giant Mothers

Black against the sky the giant mothers
are whispering together in the moonlight –
one of which, the boniest, is mine.
She stuffs my ears with centipedes and millipedes,
she crams my little mouth with bones and tongues,
she pulls my nipples in and out and beats me
with mittens made of pigskin and blood.
We never kiss. We never even try.
We never talk. She's taught me not to talk.
The things we never talk about are *private*.

She's taught me not to want what I want.
She's taught me not to hope – God forbid –
not to laugh, and not to cry in pain;
not to hear the cries of pain of others,
not to seek and not to find; she's taught me
to know my place, which is complete darkness,
where things you touch are huge beyond belief
and when you walk you need to walk on tiptoe,
circumspectly, like the slow loris
hunters trap to steal their rare eyes.

Buckets

All she does is stand there like a bucket
standing in a sort of Bucket Heaven
where nothing really matters except buckets

that stand in rows against the golden walls
with butterflies and moths
drowning in them.

Basset Hounds

On the yellow house where we're on holiday,
on the yellow hair like yellow egg,
on the yellow hands that press the eye-balls
of dreamers who can't wake from their dreams
shines the yellow light of the morning

that doesn't care how much it burns or dazzles us
or who we are or what we're doing here,
flopped inside the house in our pyjamas
like two endearingly-handmade-looking basset hounds
who haven't learned a thing about a thing.

The Pool

No one needs to know there is no pool,
no poolside bar, no guests who'll never know
it's nothing but a pool in a dream

where moonlit rubber ducks and drowned bees
that shimmer now because they shimmered then
circle in obedience to sorrow.

My Mother's Fingers

Her fingers are like snouts with which she rootles
through crannies she's no business to be rootling through;

she rootles and she grunts as if to say
life's too short for anything but rootling!

They Think They Know What Love Is

They think they know what Love is but they don't,
no one does, it is unknowable,
along with everything else, including chickens –

and anyhow how does anyone reach them,
reach my mother's cheeks, I mean?
They don't.

The Forest

Casting off her ludicrous foundation-garment
and trampling on the flower-beds as she goes,

my mother disappears into the forest
and dares me not to think I want her back.

The Giraffe

Cold beside my bed like an aeroplane
with chainsaws and prosthetics in its hold
and chained-up fish and chained-up cubes of ocean
and rectangles of ocean whose cold fish
dream of halls where terrifying fishmongers
wielding knives chop off fishes' heads
and chuck them in enormous rubber buckets
bespangled with pink blood and glittering scales,
my mother thinks she loves me but she doesn't,
she doesn't understand a word I say

and that's what makes me shout like this and stamp
and gallop round the room as if I'm galloping
round and round the shimmering savannah
with nothing in the sky above but sunshine
and nothing underfoot but cropped grass
and every time I gallop past my mother
(pressing my small lips against its neck
and telling it it's all I've ever wanted
and kissing it again and again)
I make it spit at her, which isn't kind.

Even My Huge Mother

Even my huge mother in her overcoat
locked away inside her room, is crying:
she cries all night, although you'd never know;
she cries until her mouth is stretched so tight
she turns her body inside out like laundry bags –
and, if it wasn't what she really wanted,
and what she waits all day to do, she wouldn't.

My Mother's Ankles

She neither gives nor receives love.
We don't know *why* she doesn't but she doesn't.

She runs from love like someone in a ballgown
running from morosely-crashing surf.

She runs and runs until her rippling ballgown
grabs her ankles. Happens all the time.

My Mother's Lips

They crawl across my shoulder-blades like slugs
or like the *ghosts* of slugs that have forgotten

how to be alive or who I am
or where there is to crawl to except hair.

Fairy Cakes

Not unlike the tiny cumbersome quarry-workers
that dig their way or try to dig their way
out of the rubble and ice at the end of the world
to light, to tracks, to maybe even a café
somewhere beyond the forest serving tea
and fairy cakes with sugar ducks on top,
only to die, forgotten, in their boots,

the things I tell her never reach her ears
or if they do she is too bored to listen –
bored to death! Inside her bored brain
nothing moves except a bored river
and sleepy bats the size of bumble-bees
who move as if they never move at all;
nothing moves; everything is stuck.

Rain Is Falling on the Sausages

Rain is falling on the sausages
and on the ants and on the large cows
and on the swimmer swimming in the lake
who's swimming to forget who he is,
or swimming to remember, he forgets;
who swims until he hasn't got a clue

how not to keep on swimming till he sinks
and if it's true or not that pigs can swim
and rivers always dream of being rivulets
and even those we trust can not be trusted
and light, what light there is, will start to fail
and those we love will be *chucked out* like kettlejugs.

Midges

Summer has arrived like a lorry
loaded with bright parakeets and lorikeets
and painted brilliant yellow to encourage
every little fly from miles around
to come and roast themselves on the paintwork
which bubbles just below the tiny bathroom

in which I'm busy hiding from my mother
who's catching midges
somewhere in the shrubbery
or possibly the flowerbeds although
she's really much too big for the flowerbeds
and squashes something every times she breathes.

The Dreams of Custard Creme Crumbs

Her lap is like a palace in the clouds
that I can no more climb or clamber up to

than custard creme crumbs can that can't stop dreaming
their dreams of being custard cremes again.

My Mother's Hat

In a little voice as cold as snow
I ask my mother, or my mother's hat,
just visible inside a cloud of flies
that dances round her shoulders as she wanders,
I ask my mother if it's really true –

not out loud,
not so she can hear me,
that would be too much to ask, I know that –
if it's true she loves me and my knot
of knotted silk that smells of quarried gravel.

Ruin

Please don't say they are because they're not,
they're not, they're not, I know they're not, they've ruined us,

those brutes in dresses with their long arms
and wrists like little wrists made of chickenshit.

Everyone's a Stranger

Everyone's a stranger to this world
but not so strange that it's OK to do this.

My mother is a stranger like me.
I tell myself *Don't do this*. But I do.

Happiness

My mother's throwing apples at a dog
which yaps and yaps and the more it yaps

the more my mother goes on throwing apples at it
and skidding on the apple skins. Idiots.

My Mother's Smell

If you're good you should believe in mothers
and if I'm good I should 'believe in' mine
but what does to 'believe in' something mean?

And if, each time I smell her smell, I panic,
and if that means I don't 'believe in' Love,
it doesn't, and it can't, because I do!

Sugar

Like sugar moths dissolving into sugar,
my white meringue dissolves with a puff

which blows a yellow wasp against the mouth
I used to think used to eat small children.

Lettuces

Her whimpering is getting on my nerves
but just as I'm about to shut her mouth

she falls asleep among the lettuces
as if to say *why bother standing up.*

A Visit from the Chiropodist

She's lounging on the sofa like a stranger
who's never got a kind word for anyone,
least of all a kind word for me,
a stranger in a strange and hostile country
for ever trying to find my way back home –

for where is home if home is not my mother
who all this time is lounging on the sofa
refusing to acknowledge the chiropodist
whose smile is as sweet as an almond
embedded in a golden macaroon?

Ice Veil

She's going to have to learn to try and tell me
things she'd rather not,
private things,
things she doesn't even know herself
and doesn't want to know or even think about,
she's going to have to try and learn to touch me,
touch my cheek, as if we were normal;

as if our hearts were whole and not broken;
as if she wasn't lost inside these tears
that elongate themselves like long rabbits
hanging by their paws from a hook
until they form a veil of brown ice
that can't remember what it feels like
or used to feel like to have been warm.

My Mother's Yard

I park the car in the parking place
and walk across the yard in the rain.

My mother's in the shed chopping wood.
Pity us. We don't know what to say.

The Box

Trembling with what ought to be forgiveness –
which always sounds so beautiful, doesn't it?-
trembling like a man who loves a woman

who creeps into his bedroom out of nowhere
and strokes a knife across his trembling throat:
trembling like a box in which a head –

a single human head that can't speak
and crawls with flies and soaks the cardboard walls
with roses of dark blood that seep reluctantly

from underneath its eyeless sequinned sleeping-mask –
trembles on the chair beside her bed,
I'm praying she will never wake up.

The Gold Hotel

She hangs, or what she wants to tell me hangs,
far beyond my reach like a songbird
for ever sealed in a chandelier

that God Himself could not be heard inside
and if I knew what she knows – which I don't,
she hardly knows herself, no one should,

she keeps it hidden like a gold hotel
she's carried to the bed of the sea
and buried there, embracing solitude –

if I knew, and even if I don't,
because her words say one thing and her eyes
say something else, I know I'll never leave her.

Junk

All my mother's repulsive boarded junk –
not only in the filthy upstairs bedrooms
but even in the drawing-room downstairs
so nobody's got anywhere to sit,
you try to find a chair, it's choc-a-bloc,
she's squatting there knee-deep in all this junk

while thinking (and this really does my head in!)
thinking she's knee-deep in precious jewels –
all this junk of hers is *in the way*
and nobody can move, far less *dance*,
and anyone who's ever danced will know
that dancing is *the only way forward*!

Daddylonglegs

They need to be alone and a man
bursting in like this ruins everything

and anyone who thinks that daddylonglegs
are *harmless little things* can eff off.

How to Float

Forgive ourselves, that's all we can do,
although we don't know what forgiveness is

or how to coax it out into the light
or what it is we're coaxing it to do

or not to do, or how to be ashamed;
how not to lose our minds, how to float.

Some Dreams Are Made of Fog

Some dreams are made of fog and some of lace
and some of someone calling her again
down the hall and past the gladioli
and out onto the road where a lorry

loaded with the corpses of white lambs
swerves into the lounge to avoid her
and splat into the arms of the doctor
who's come to give her *her little injection* again.

Chicken Soup

Her chicken soup is waiting in the dining-room
but all she wants to do is lie down

and go to Heaven where the angels sing
and everyone who wants to cry can do so.

In My Mother's Bathroom

Day and night she washes and she washes –
or should that be she scrubs and she scrubs? –
behind the ears, between the legs, everywhere,

but actually *she wants to be dirty!*
Very very dirty. My mother
wants to be disgusting. We all do.

Toad

Once a toad peered between the bars,
only to flap off without a word,

leaving her alone in her room
making her unnerving little gulping noises.

Birds in Coats

Neither of us knows a thing about it
or what we have to do to actually do it

so neither of us does it and we sit here
like birds in coats that don't know how to fly.

Hospitalisation

They roll her out of bed like a sack
(full of babies, I was going to say –

squashed together so they can't breathe
and think they're going to die and they are,

I'm sorry, but they are – but I won't)
they roll her like a sack of potatocs.

Dragonfly

It's fun to have it riding on my nose
even if it doesn't know I'm here

tiptoeing along in my boots
trying to impersonate a water-lily!

My Mother's Upper Lip Area

Chilly to the touch like margarine,
my mother's upper lip produces hairs

the way old margarine produces hairs
(although the hairs of margarine are softer).

My Mother's Eyes

She smiles but she really wants to die!
You see it in her eyes.

It doesn't matter.
I tell myself she's just an old bag.

The Dusty Gnu

My mother, like a gnu with glass eyes,
stares at me as if she can't remember me –

can't or won't: like a dusty gnu
the only thing she really likes is boredom!

My Mother's Eiderdown

Spare a little love for the balding,
spare a little love for the sick,

spare a little love for the eiderdown
she grips so tight, and for the eider duck.

My Mother's Smile

Because she can't be bothered to smile
even at her son I now know

my mother has become an old woman
and other things are more important to her.

Someone in a Bath Towel

Someone in a bath-towel
with meringues

his mother made
is trying not to cry.

Cottage Pie

Wrap me up and roll me underground
somewhere where there's nowhere I can stop
and no one is allowed to come near me
and I can laugh until my hoots of laughter
echo through the tunnels like the wind;
somewhere underground where potatoes
sent by God for making cottage pie with,
with lots of butter, lots of hot milk,
salt and pepper, obviously, and nutmeg,
and beetroot if you've got it, or tomatoes,
or cochineal – wow, cochineal! –
will shelter me inside their cool potato-beds,

O take me somewhere I can laugh my head off
and never stop until a band of angels
scoops me up, still hooting, and I'm begging them
please to turn me please into an owl
and please can I have wings and be invisible
and please can I be saved from my mother
and please can she be washed and disinfected
and also please disinfect her sponge-bag
and everything inside her sponge-bag, Mamma,
please don't raise your voice like this, remember
and please don't do this to me, please don't do this,
my name is Sunshine, take me away.

The Only Thing I Eat

The only thing I eat is my Panadol.
Otherwise everything is liquidised.

The Panadol I crush between two spoons
until it has a satin-like consistency.

And sometimes I will lick or suck at jelly buttons.
Don't ask me why but I refuse to chew.

How Sweet the Name

My mother has become an old woman
who can't remember names, even hers;

whose name is now nothing but 'my mother';
who sweet the name of sheep may safely graze.

Man with a Grasshopper on His Nose

At the very moment when my mother,
bored of breathing in and breathing out,
finally decides not to bother,

a grasshopper hops onto my nose
who thinks it's not a nose but a hilltop,
motionless against the red sun.

ACKNOWLEDGEMENTS

My thanks are due to the editors of the following publicatior in whose pages some of these poems first appeared: *Artemi Best British Poetry 2012*, ed. Sasha Dugdale & Roddy Lumsd((Salt Publishing, 2012), *Granta, Magma, Mountain Silence, Mslexia, The North, Poetry Daily* (USA), *Poetry London* and *Poetry Review*; to the organisers and judges of the Flarestack, Mslexia, National Poetry and Second Light Poetry Competitions and of the Michael Marks Award; also to the Arvon Foundation, the Southbank Centre, London, the School of English at the University of Exeter, and to Harvard University's Center for Hellenic Studies in Olympia for their exceptional hospitality.

I would also like to offer special thanks to Claire Leech and Barbara Preston at Lyme Regis library for their unfailing help and good humour; to Tom Battye; to Lorna Jenkin; to Alisoun; to Steve Jarvis; to Pearl Esther Hill (who likes meatballs); to Mike (I hope he knows which Mike he is); to the late David Foster Wallace for the phrase 'the lovely scent of illegally burned leaves', and lastly, and for very different reasons, to R.H.H., although whether alive or dead I can never be sure.

Finally, I would like to add that the sequence 'Into My Mother's Snow-Encrusted Lap' is not about my own mother. Far from it.